SATIE for the Guitar

Erik Satie's Piano Pieces

3 Gymnopedies
and
3 Gnossiennes

Transcribed for Guitar
by PETER CHARLES KRAUS

ED-2940

ISBN 0-7935-5543-4

G. SCHIRMER, Inc.

DISTRIBUTED BY

HAL•LEONARD®
CORPORATION

7777 W. BLUEMOUND RD. P.O. BOX 13819 MILWAUKEE, WI 53213

NOTE

The notational system I have used in these transcriptions is the same as that employed by Theodore Norman. Mr. Norman's introduction to his "Music for the Guitar Soloist" is included in this publication by permission of the publisher.

P.K.

FOR THE PLAYER

I = 1st string, E
II = 2nd string, B
III = 3rd string, G
IV = 4th string, D
V = 5th string, A
VI = 6th string, E

Look at the first piece; the ROMAN NUMERALS you see refer to the string you are to play on. You continue to play on this Roman numeral-marked string until the next Roman numeral is given.

In this volume, the pieces run the gamut of the whole guitar keyboard.

By learning to use the proper approach to "box" indentication, you will learn that the beginner playing in the first 5 boxes of the guitar has already learned to play in the most awkward part of the guitar keyboard.

From the 6th box through the 14th and upward, the boxes get smaller and the left hand moves with greater ease.

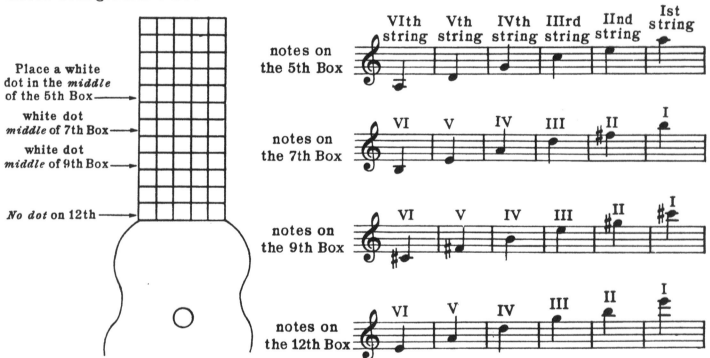

You will learn the notes on either side of the 5th box by inference.

Example:

Since A is in the 5th box on the VIth string

G♯ or A♭ is in the 4th box on the VIth string

Example:

Since A is in the 5th box on the VIth string

A♯ or B♭ is in the 6th box on the VIth string

Three Gymnopedies *

Transcribed by Peter Kraus

Erik Satie

1

Lent et douloureaux (Slowly and mournfully)

* Ceremonial choral dances performed at ancient Greek festivals.

47249c

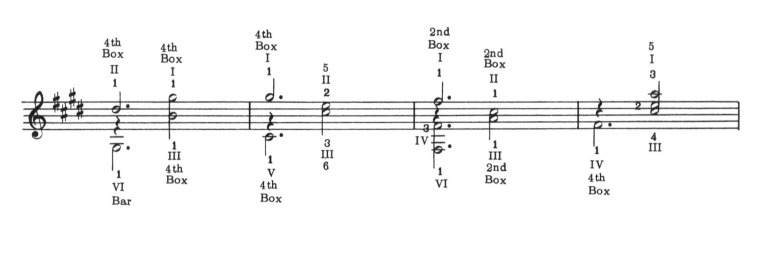

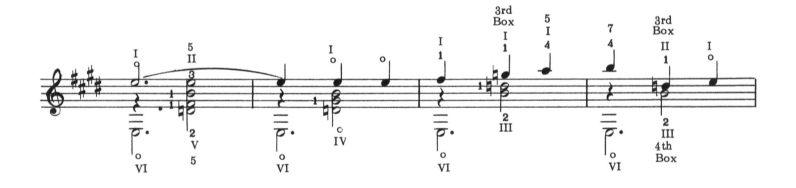

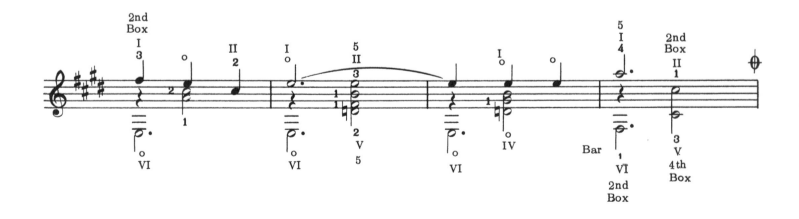

CODA

D. C. al ⊕ al Coda

2

Lent et triste (Slowly and sadly)

3

Lent et grave (Slowly and solemnly)

Three Gnossiennes*

Transcribed by Peter Kraus

Erik Satie

1

VI = D

Lent (Slowly)

second time : très luisant (very brightly)

* The title is most likely a vague allusion to Cnossus, Knossos, or Gnossos, an ancient city on the island of Crete – the site of the palace of the mythical King Minos and the labyrinth where the Minotaur was confined–richly associated in ancient Greek mythology with Jupiter, Ariadne, and Theseus, the hero who slew the Minotaur.

47249c

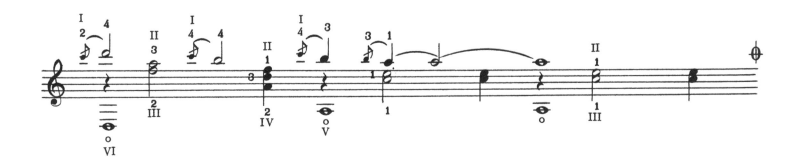

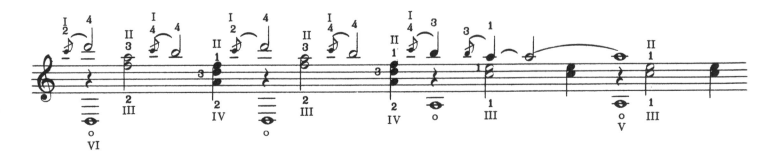

du bout de la pensée (on the edge of an idea)

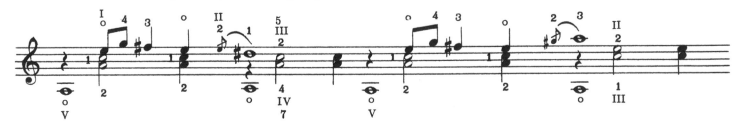

Dal ℅ al ⊕ al Coda

sur la langue (on the tip of the tongue)

CODA

2

VI = E

Avec étonnement (With astonishment)

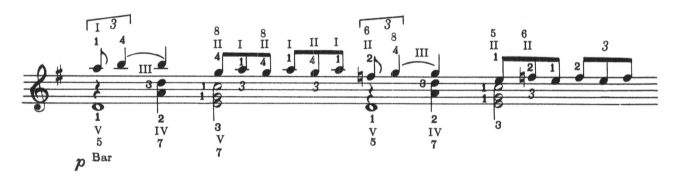

p Bar

ne sortez pas (don't leave)

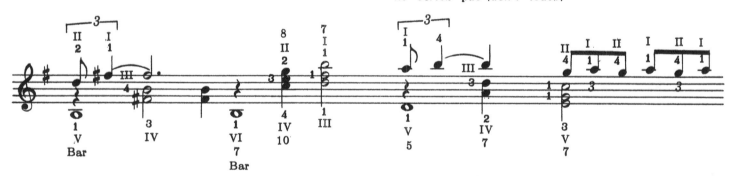

Bar

Bar

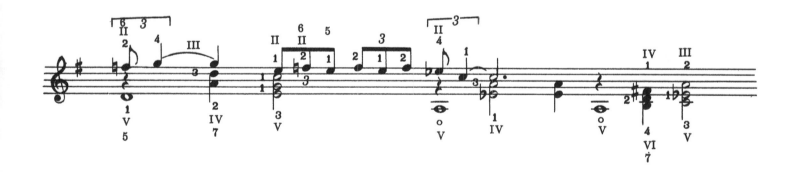

14

dans une grande bonté (with great kindness)

plus intimement (more intimately)

avec une légère intimité (with a light intimacy)

sans orgueil (without arrogance)

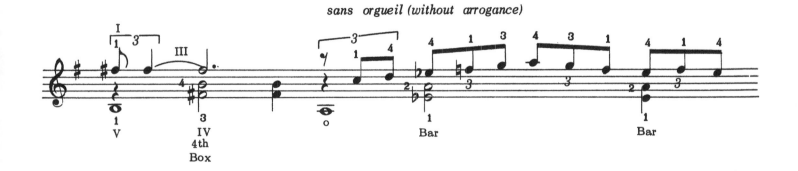

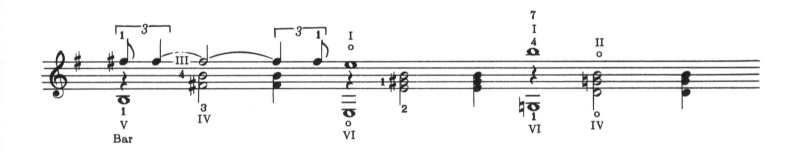

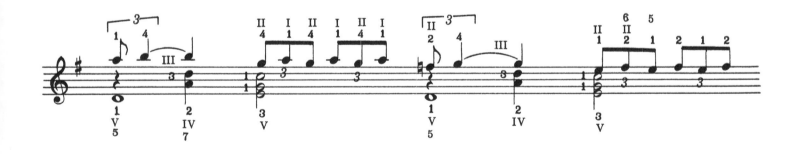

3

Lent (Slowly)

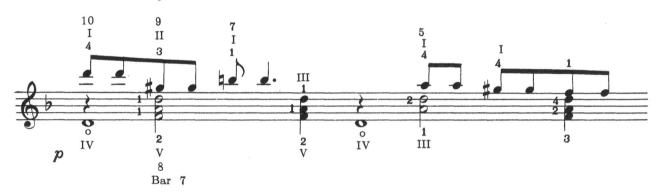

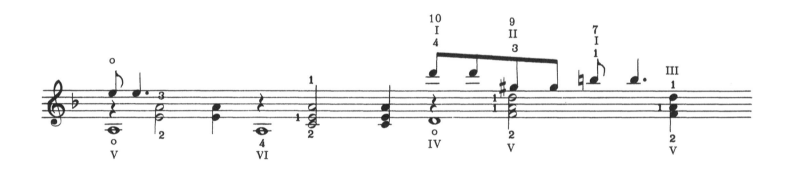

conseillez – vous soigneusement (plan with care)

*munissez-vous de clairvoyance
(arm yourself with perspicacity)*

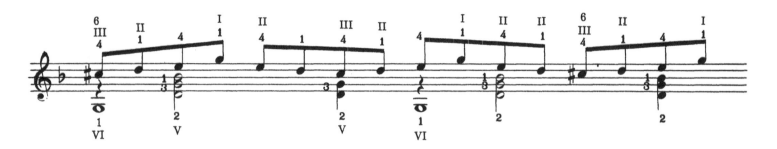

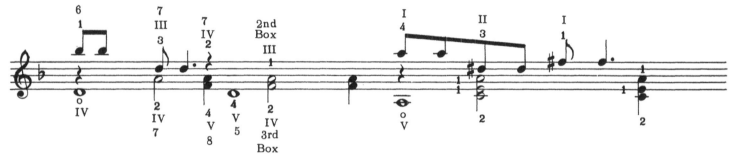

seul, pendant une instant(alone, for a moment)

de manier à obtenir un creux (how to achieve absolutely nothing)

très perdu (quite lost)

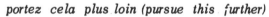

portez cela plus loin (pursue this further)

ouvrez la tête (open your head)

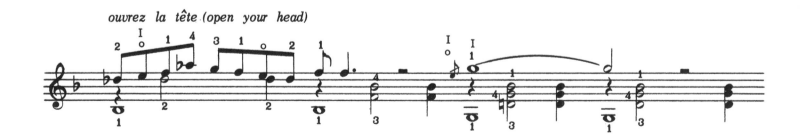

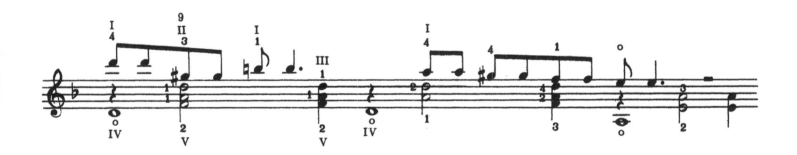

enfouissez le son (muffle the sound)

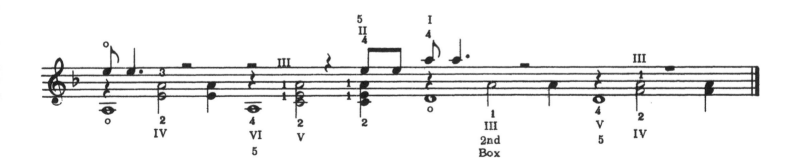